VOCAL SOLO

Solos For K

HLE
HAL LEONARD EUROPE
DISTRIBUTED BY MUSIC SALES

Published by
Hal Leonard Europe
A Music Sales / Hal Leonard Joint Venture Company
14-15 Berners Street, London W1T 3LJ, UK.

Exclusive Distributors:
Music Sales Limited
Distribution Centre, Newmarket Road, Bury St Edmunds, Suffolk IP33 3YB, UK.

Order No. HLE90004376

ISBN 978-1-61780-456-4

Your Guarantee of Quality
As publishers, we strive to produce every book to the highest commercial standards.
The book has been carefully designed to minimise awkward page turns and to make playing from it a real pleasure.
Throughout, the printing and binding have been planned to ensure a sturdy, attractive publication which should give years of enjoyment.
If your copy fails to meet our high standards, please inform us and we will gladly replace it.

www.musicsales.com

Contents

Pianists on the CD:
[1] Louise Lerch
[2] Lawrence Yurman

CANDLE ON THE WATER

from Walt Disney's *Pete's Dragon*

Words and Music by Al Kasha
and Joel Hirschhorn

Smoothly

B♭ C C7 Fsus F B♭ C C7
A cold and friend-less tide has found you, don't let the storm-y dark-ness
F Gm7 F Am7 D7 G
pull you down. I'll paint a ray of hope a-round you,
F Em/G F B♭6/9 G7
cir-cling in the air light-ed by a prayer.
C Dm G7 F G C Am F
I'll be your can-dle on the wa-ter, this flame in-side of me will

B♭ G E/G♯ Am C7/G F C/E
grow. Keep hold - ing on, you'll make it, here's my hand so take it.
F G7 C C7 F Fm C F♯m7♭5 F6 G7
Look for me reach-ing out to show as sure as riv-ers flow, I'll nev-er let you
rit.
a tempo
C G F G7 C G F G7
go, I'll nev-er let you go, I'll nev-er let you
C G/B F/A C/G G C
go.

GETTING TO KNOW YOU

from *The King And I*

Lyrics by Oscar Hammerstein II
Music by Richard Rodgers

Edim7 B♭/F G9 Gm7/C Gm7
learn - ing (You'll for - give me if I boast.) And I've now be - come an
C9 Cm7/F (Spoken) F7
ex - pert On the sub - ject I like most, Get-ting to know you.
Refrain (gracefully and not fast)
B♭ Cm7(add4) F7
Get-ting to know you, get-ting to know all a - bout you
mp tranquillo
Cm7(add4) F7 Cm7 F7 Cm7 F7 B♭
Get-ting to like you, get-ting to hope you like me

E♭maj7 E♭6
Get-ting to know you, Put-ting it my way, but nice - ly
E♭+ E♭ Gm7(add4) C7 Cm7/F
You are pre-cise - ly My cup of tea!
cresc.
mf
F7 B♭ Cm7(add4) F7
Get-ting to know you, get-ting to feel free and eas - y
f
p
Cm7(add4) F7 Cm7 F7 Cm7 F7 B♭7
When I am with you, get-ting to know what to say.

E♭maj7 E♭6 Cm7 F7
Have-n't you no - ticed? Sud - den - ly I'm bright and
B♭maj7 B♭7 E♭maj7 B♭
breez - y Be - cause of all the
Cm7 F7sus F7 B♭6(add9) Gm7 C7 Gm7 C7
beau - ti - ful and new things I'm learn - ing a - bout you
poco a poco cresc.
Cm7 F7 B♭ E♭ B♭
day by day.
mf

HIGH HOPES

from the Frank Capra film *A Hole In The Head*

Words by Sammy Cahn
Music by James Van Heusen
Arranged by Michael Dansicker

B♭9 B♭7 E♭ Edim7
think he'll move that rub - ber tree plant. an - y - one knows an
Fm7 F♯dim7 Fm7 B♭7 E♭6 B♭/D E♭7 A♭ A♭maj7
ant can't move a rub - ber tree plant, but he's got high
rit.
a tempo
mf
A♭6 Adim7 E♭/B♭ E♭maj7 E♭6 Cm7 F7 Cm7 F7
hopes, he's got high hopes, he's got high ap - ple
Cm7/F F7 B♭ B♭7 E♭
pie in the sky hopes. So an - y time you're get - tin' low,

E♭/D♭
A♭/C
A dim7
'stead - of let - tin' go, just re - mem - ber that ant!
E♭6
E dim7
Fm7
B♭6
B♭7add9
E♭6
E dim7
Fm7
B♭6
B♭7add9
Oops! There goes an - oth - er rub - ber tree Oops! There goes an - oth - er rub - ber tree
E♭
E dim7
Fm7
B♭6
G7/B
Cm
E♭/B♭
F7
Oops! There goes an - oth - er rub - ber tree plant!
Fm7
B♭9
E♭
B♭
E♭
There goes an - oth - er rub - ber tree plant! Ker - plop!
3
3
sfz

I'D DO ANYTHING

from the Broadway Musical *Oliver!*

Words and Music by
Lionel Bart

This song is performed by The Artful Dodger, Nancy, Oliver Twist, Bet and Fagin in the show, adapted here as a solo.

Gm7 B♭ Cm Cm7 F7 F+
an - y - where for your smile, an - y - where, for
B♭ B♭maj7 Dm Gm Gm7 Cm7
your smile ev - 'ry - where I'd see.
F7 B♭ Gm Cm7 F7
Would you lace my shoe? An - y - thing! Paint your
Would you rob a shop? An - y - thing! Would you
Cm7 F7 B♭ E♭
face bright blue? An - y - thing! Catch a kan - ga - roo?
risk "the drop"? An - y - thing! Tho' your eyes go "pop"?

* *When singing this song as a solo, this phrase in parentheses should probably be omitted.*

MY FAVORITE THINGS
from *The Sound Of Music*

Lyrics by Oscar Hammerstein II
Music by Richard Rodgers

Em
Cream - col - ored po - nies and crisp ap - ple
mf
mp
Cmaj7
stru - dels, Door - bells and sleigh - bells and schnitz - el with noo - dles,
Am7
D7
G/B
C/E
G/D
Wild geese that fly with the moon on their wings, These are a
C
F♯m7♭5
B7
E
few of my fa - vor - ite things.
f

A
Girls in white dress - es with blue sat - in sash - es, Snow - flakes that
mf
Am7 D7
stay on my nose and eye - lash - es, Sil - ver white win - ters that
G/B C/E G/D C F♯m7♭5 B7♭9
melt in - to springs, These are a few of my fa - vor - ite things.
Em F♯m7♭5 B7 Em
When the dog bites, When the bee stings, When I'm
mf

C
feel - ing sad, I sim - ply re - mem - ber my
A7/C♯ A7 G/D C/D G/D C/D G D7♭9
fa - vor - ite things and then I don't feel
cresc.
D13 G B7♭9 G
so bad. bad.
f
f
C G/D D7 G
sf

PART OF YOUR WORLD

from Walt Disney's *The Little Mermaid*

Music by Alan Menken
Lyrics by Howard Ashman

B♭ C/B♭ B♭
Look at this trove, treas - ures un - told. How man - y won - ders can
C/B♭ Am7 Dm7
one cav - ern hold? Look - ing a - round here you'd think, sure, she's got
F/G G7 B♭maj7
ev - 'ry - thing. I've got gad - gets and giz - mos a -
Am7 F/A Dm7 F/G G7
plen - ty. I've got who - zits and what - zits ga - lore. You want

B♭maj7
3
thing - a - ma - bobs, I've got
Am7 F/A
twen - ty. But who
Dm7
cares? No big
rall.
F/G G7
deal. I want
B♭/C Am/C
more.
a tempo
B♭/C C7
F
I wan - na be where the
a tempo
Am7
peo - ple are.
B♭
I wan - na see wan - na
B♭/C C
see 'em danc - in',
Dm
walk - in' a - round on those,
Am
what - d' - ya call 'em, oh,

B♭/C
C
C7
F
feet.
Flip - pin' your fins you don't
F/A
B♭
B♭/C
C
get too far.
Legs are re - quired for jump - in', danc - in'.
Dm
Am
F/A
B♭/C
Stroll - in' a - long down the, what's that word a - gain, street.
C7
F
F/E♭
Up where they walk, up where they run, up where they

B♭/D
stay all day in the sun.
B♭m/D♭
Wan - der - in'
F/C
free, wish I could
B♭/C
be
C
part of that
F
world.
What would I
B♭
give if I could
C/B♭
live out - ta these
Am
wa - ters.
Dm
What would I
B♭
pay to spend a
C/B♭
day warm on the

Am
F7sus
F7
B♭
sand. Bet - cha on land they un - der -
C/B♭
A7sus
A7
Dm
Dm/C
stand. Bet they don't re - pri - mand their daugh - ters. Bright young
F/G
G
F/G
G
E♭maj7
wom - en, sick of swim - min' read - y to stand.
rall.
a tempo
B♭/C
C
B♭/C
C
F
F/A
And read - y to know what the peo - ple know.

B♭maj7
B♭/C
Ask 'em my ques - tions and get some an - swers.
Dm
Am
F/A
What's a fire, and why does it, what's the word,
Gm7
C7
F
3
burn. When's it my turn? Would - n't I
F/E♭
B♭/D
B♭m/D♭
love, love to ex - plore that shore up a - bove,

out of the sea.
Wish I could
slower
F
Bb/C
C7
Bb
be part of that world.
L.H.
C/Bb
Bb
C/Bb
F

THE RAINBOW CONNECTION

from *The Muppet Movie*

Words and Music by Paul Williams
and Kenneth L. Ascher

A E/G♯ F♯m7 A/E D(add2) D(add2)/A
rain - bows have noth - ing to hide.
look what it's done so far.
Dmaj7
So we've been told, and some choose to be - lieve it.
What's so a - maz - ing that keeps us star - gaz - ing, and
G♯m/C♯
I know they're wrong; wait and see.
what do we think we might see?
Bm7 E D/E C♯m7 E/F♯ F♯7
Some - day we'll find it, the Rain - bow Con - nec - tion; the
Some - day we'll find it, the Rain - bow Con - nec - tion; the

1
Bm7 E7sus E7 A D/A
lov - ers, the dream - ers, and me.
lov - ers, the dream - ers, and
A D/A
2
A E/G♯
me. All of us
F♯m7 A/E D(add2) A/C♯
un - der its spell; we know that it's prob - a - bly
D6/E E♭6/F F(add2) F B♭(add2)
mag - ic. Have you been

F/G Gm7 Cm7 Eb/F F Bb F/A
half a - sleep and have you heard voic - es? I've heard them
Gm7 Bb/F Eb(add2) Eb/F Fsus Bb F/G Gm7
call - ing my name. Is this the sweet sound that
Cm7 Eb/F F Bb F/A Gm7 Eb(add2)
calls the young sail - ors? The voice might be one and the same.
Eb Ebmaj7
I've heard it too man - y times to ig -

Am/D
nore it. It's some - thing that I'm s'posed to be.
Cm7 F E♭/F Dm7 F/G G7
Some - day we'll find it, the Rain - bow Con - nec - tion; the
Cm7 F7sus F7 B♭ F/A Gm7
lov - ers the dream-ers, and me. La da da dee da da
B♭/F E♭(add2) E♭ Fsus F7 B♭
do la la da da da de da do.
L.H.

WE'RE ALL IN THIS TOGETHER

from the Disney Channel Original Movie *High School Musical*

Words and Music by Matthew Gerrard
and Robbie Nevil

D♭
time for cel - e - bra - tion.
E♭
I fi - n'lly fig - ured
D♭
out,
yeah, yeah,
E♭
that all our dreams
D♭
have no lim - i - ta - tions;
E♭
that's what it's all a - bout.
D♭
E♭
(C'-mon, now.)
F N.C.
Ev - 'ry - one
is
E♭
spe - cial in their own way;
F
we make each oth - er
E♭
strong.
F
We're not the same;
we're

E♭ F E♭ F
dif-f'rent in a good way. To-geth-er's where we be - long. We're
G D/F♯ Em G/D C G/B
all in this to-geth - er; once we know that we are, we're all stars,
C/E D/F♯ G D/F♯ Em G/D
and we see that. We're all in this to-geth - er; and it shows
C G/B C/E D/F♯ F5
when we stand hand in hand, make our dreams come true.

G
Ev - 'ry - bod - y now: To - geth - er, to - geth - er,
To - geth - er, we're there for
F G
to - geth - er, ev - 'ry - one. To - geth - er, to - geth - er,
each oth - er ev - 'ry time. To - geth - er, to - geth - er,
1 F
c' - mon, let's have some fun.
2 F
c' - mon, let's do this right. We're
G D/F♯ Em G/D C G/B
all in this to - geth - er; once we know that we are, we're all stars,
all in this to - geth - er; when we reach, we can fly, know in - side
f

C/E D/F♯ G D/F♯ Em G/D
and we see that. We're all in this to - geth - er; and it shows
we can make it. We're all in this to - geth - er; once we see
C G/B
when we stand hand in hand, make our dreams come... We're
there's a chance that we have,
1
C/E D/F♯
2
C/E D/F♯
and we take it.
F
Wild cats ev - 'ry - where, wave your hands up in the air.
That's the way we do it; let's get to it, c' - mon ev - 'ry - one!
G

STEPSISTERS' LAMENT

from *Cinderella*

Lyrics by Oscar Hammerstein II
Music by Richard Rodgers

Dm7 G7 Dm G7 C(add2) C Cmaj7/G C6
bub - ble with a flim-sy kind of charm, And with ver - y lit - tle
Am7 D9/A B7 Em G7♯9 G7
trou - ble I could break her lit - tle arm! Oh, oh,
C F Dm7 C/G G13 G7
why would a fel - low want a girl like her, So ob - vious - ly un - u - sual?
C F Dm7 C/E G7 C
Why can't a fel - low ev - er once pre - fer a u - sual girl like me? Her

F C F Adim7/E C
cheeks are a pret-ty shade of pink, But not an-y pink-er than a rose is. Her
F C Am D7 G7♯9 G7 C7
skin may be del-i-cate and soft, But not an-y soft-er than a doe's is. Her
F C F Adim7/E C
neck is no whit-er than a swan's. She's on-ly as dain-ty as a dai-sy. She's
F C Am D7 G7♯11 G7
on-ly as grace-ful as a bird. So why is the fel-low go-ing cra-zy? Oh,

C F Dm7 C/G
why would a fel - low want a girl like her, a girl who's mere - ly
G13 G7 C F Dm7
love - ly? Why can't a fel - low ev - er once pre - fer a
C E7/G♯ Am Dm9
girl who's mere - ly me? What's the mat - ter with the man? What's the mat - ter with the
G13 C
man? What's the mat - ter with the man?

WHO WILL BUY?

from the Broadway Musical *Oliver!*

Words and Music by
Lionel Bart

This song is performed by Oliver Twist and Chorus in the show, adapted here as a solo.

Dm
Gm7
A7
Dm
Who will tie it up with a rib - bon, and
Gm7
Gm7/C
F
put it in a box for me?
So I can
There'll nev - er
Gm
Gm7
C7♭9
Fmaj7
F6
F
F6
see it at my lei - sure when -
be a day so sun - ny; it
Gm
Gm7
C7♭9
Fmaj7
F6
ev - er things go wrong, and I would
could not hap - pen twice. Where is the

Am7 C/G F#m7b5 B7b9 Em
keep it as a treas - ure to
man with all the mon - ey? It's
Am Am/G F7 E7#5 A7b9 A7 A7b9 A7
last my whole life long.
cheap at half the price!
Dm Gm7 A7 Dm
Who will buy this won - der - ful feel - ing?
Gm7 Em7 A
I'm so high, I swear I could fly.

Dm
Gm7 A7 Dm
Me, oh, my, I don't want to lose it, so
Gm7 Gm7/C F6 F7
what am I to do, to keep the sky so blue? There
B♭ A7♯5 A7
1
Dm
must be some - one who will buy.
2
Dm Gm Em7♭5 Dm
buy.

About the Enhanced CD

In addition to full performances and piano accompaniments playable on both your CD player and computer, the enhanced CD also includes tempo adjustment and transposition software for computer use only. This software, known as Amazing Slow Downer, was originally created for use in pop music to allow singers and players the freedom to independently adjust both tempo and pitch elements. Because we believe there may be valuable uses for these features in other musical genres, we have included this software as a tool for both the teacher and student. For quick and easy installation instructions of this software, please see below.

In recording a piano accompaniment we necessarily must choose one tempo. Our choice of tempo, phrasing and dynamics is carefully considered. But by the nature of recording, it is only one option.

However, we encourage you to explore your own interpretive ideas, which may differ from our recordings. This new software feature allows you to adjust the tempo up and down without affecting the pitch. Likewise, Amazing Slow Downer allows you to shift pitch up and down without affecting the tempo. We recommend that these new tempo and pitch adjustment features be used with care and insight.

The audio quality may be somewhat compromised when played through the Amazing Slow Downer. This compromise in quality will not be a factor in playing the CD audio track on a normal CD player or through another audio computer program.

INSTALLATION FROM DOWNLOAD:

For Windows (XP, Vista or 7):

1. Download and save the .zip file to your hard drive.
2. Extract the .zip file.
3. Open the "ASD Lite" folder.
4. Double-click "setup.exe" to run the installer and follow the on-screen instructions.

For Macintosh (OSX 10.4 and up):

1. Download and save the .dmg file to your hard drive.
2. Double-click the .dmg file to mount the "ASD Lite" volume.
3. Double-click the "ASD Lite" volume to see its contents.
4. Drag the "ASD Lite" application into the Application folder.

INSTALLATION FROM CD:

For Windows (XP, Vista or 7):

1. Load the CD-ROM into your CD-ROM drive.
2. Open your CD-ROM drive. You should see a folder named "Amazing Slow Downer." If you only see a list of tracks, you are looking at the audio portion of the disk and most likely do not have a multi-session capable CD-ROM.
3. Open the "Amazing Slow Downer" folder.
4. Double-click "setup.exe" to install the software from the CD-ROM to your hard disk. Follow the on-screen instructions to complete installation.
5. Go to "Start," "Programs" and find the "Amazing Slow Downer Lite" application. Note: To guarantee access to the CD-ROM drive, the user should be logged in as the "Administrator."

For Macintosh (OSX 10.4 or higher):

1. Load the CD-ROM into your CD-ROM drive.
2. Double-click on the data portion of the CD-ROM (which will have the Hal Leonard icon in red and be named as the book).
3. Open the "Amazing OSX" folder.
4. Double-click the "ASD Lite" application icon to run the software from the CD-ROM, or copy this file to your hard drive and run it from there.

MINIMUM SOFTWARE REQUIREMENTS:

For Windows (XP, Vista or 7):
Pentium Processor; Windows XP, Vista, or 7; 8 MB Application RAM; 8x Multi-Session CD-ROM drive

For Macintosh (OSX 10.4 or higher):
Power Macintosh or Intel Processor; Mac OSX 10.4 or higher; MB Application RAM; 8x Multi-Session CD-ROM drive